Bikini

HAMLYN

Editor: Mike Evans
Production Controller: Melanie Frantz
Picture Research: Wendy Gay
Art Director: Keith Martin
Design: Valerie Hawthorn

Consultant Editor: Emily Evans

First published in 1996 by Hamlyn,
an imprint of Reed Consumer Books Limited,
Michelin House, 81 Fulham Road,
London SW3 6RB
and Auckland, Melbourne, Singapore and Toronto

A Catalogue record for this book is available from the British Library
ISBN 0 600 58984 6

Printed and bound in Singapore

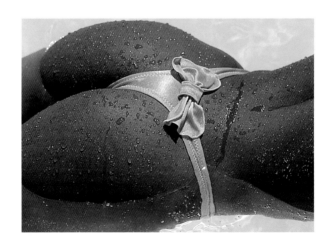

G. Hooman
2/1/97

contents

Bikini.

South Sea islands...palm trees swaying in the breeze...the heat haze shimmering on the still surface of blue lagoon waters...a tropical sky glowing brighter than a thousand suns...the mind-boggling impact on an unsuspecting world...

...and that was only the atom bomb...

THE
BIRTH
OF
THE
Bikini

ALTHOUGH TWO-PIECE BATHING SUITS HAD APPEARED

DURING THE PREVIOUS DECADE, WITH THE LOWER HALF BEING

BASICALLY SHORTS, THERE'S A THEORY THAT THE AMERICAN

GOVERNMENT DURING THE SECOND

WORLD WAR SHOULD

BE THANKED FOR THE PROMOTION OF

THE TWO-PIECE WHEN IN 1943 IT DEEMED THAT FABRIC

USED IN WOMEN'S SWIMWEAR SHOULD BE REDUCED BY 10%

FOR AUSTERITY REASONS, THEREFORE REMOVING FIRST THE

'SKIRT' PANEL ON A ONE-PIECE GARMENT THEN THE MIDRIFF

TOO – THE MODERN TWO PIECE WAS BORN.

bikini atoll

THREE YEARS LATER, ON JUNE 30TH 1946, THE AMERICAN NUCLEAR

TEST CARRIED OUT ON BIKINI ATOLL IN THE SOUTH PACIFIC INSPIRED

A PARIS DESIGNER, LOUIS RÉARD, TO DUB HIS LATEST – AND FOR

THE TIME EXTREMELY MINIMAL – SWIMWEAR DESIGN 'THE BIKINI'.

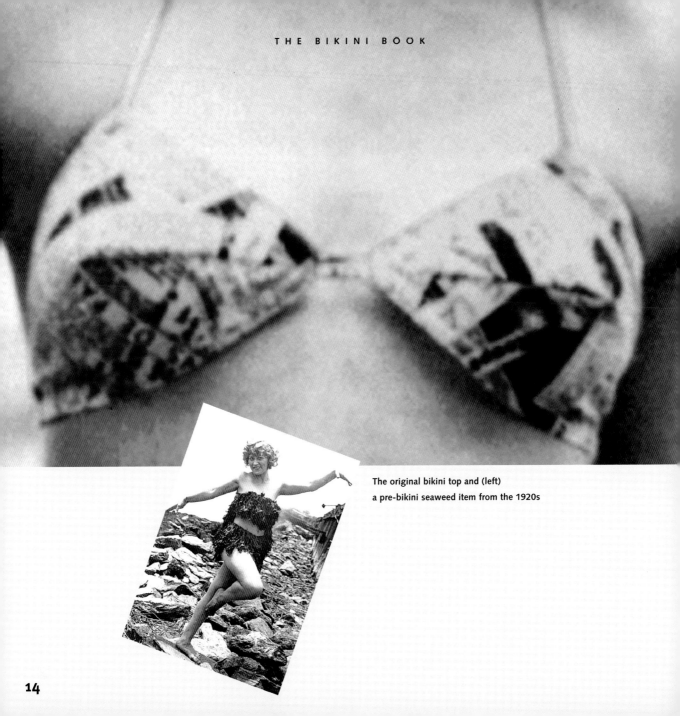

The original bikini top and (left)
a pre-bikini seaweed item from the 1920s

The

style was simultaneously

introduced by a better-known designer Jacques

Heim who had dubbed his creation the *atome*, but the

nuclear tests provided Réard with a name that was to

capture the public's imagination and become a

part of international language. The minimalist

swimsuit was modelled by Micheline

Bernardini, a nude dancer from the Casino

de Paris revue show, on July 5th 1946, and

was an immediate media sensation

world-wide.

Réard (top) and Micheline Bernardini

STARS & STARLETS

A youthful Brigitte Bardot (top left), starlet Eve Daves (bottom left) and Nicole Maurey, all making the most of the Cannes photocalls

The Bikini took off in France, where
it was created, before anywhere else,
and by the 1950s had been adopted by
the rest of the world, largely through
the hype-potential it presented to the
film industry. Significantly, it was
again in France where this
initially materialised. The annual
Cannes Film Festival became, in the
early 50s, the international launching pad
not just for new films, but a galaxy of
budding female stars, whose studios
arranged as many photo opportunities
on the sun-kissed beaches of the
Cote D'Azure as possible.

The bikini of course was invaluable in all this. France's own superstar of the era, Brigitte Bardot, made the bikini-look her own, and made her base down the coast at St Tropez equally fashionable at the same time. In seminal shockers like 'And God Created Woman' (1956) the ultimate sex kitten helped revolutionise the cinema's attitude to bare flesh.

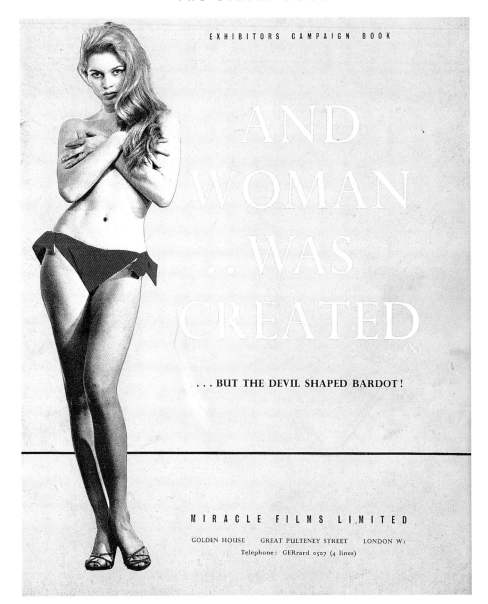

EXHIBITORS CAMPAIGN BOOK

AND
WOMAN
... WAS
CREATED
(X)

... BUT THE DEVIL SHAPED BARDOT!

MIRACLE FILMS LIMITED

GOLDEN HOUSE   GREAT PULTENEY STREET   LONDON W1
Telephone : GERrard 0597 (4 lines)

Promotional material for the UK release of 'And God Created Woman', with its modified British title

BB

MICHEL BOISROND'S "WOMEN ARE WEAK"   Also known as "FAIBLES FEMMES" in French
starring MYLENE DEMONGEOT · PASCALE PETIT · JACQUELINE SASSARD and ALAIN DELON
A PAUL GRAETZ Production . . . in Eastman Color   A Paramount Release

Among the many continental film actresses whose careers were
launched, though not always successfully, via bikini shots, were the
French starlets Liliane Brousse (left) and Mylene Demongeot.

Illustrator Al Moore was a major contributor to America's Esquire magazine in the 1950s

Meanwhile, stars from all over the world took to the promenade and beach at Cannes and other Mediterranean resorts in the skimpiest of two-pieces in front of the world's cameras. British stars and starlets who found the bikini a publicity boon included Joan Collins (right, and in the insert with her sister Jackie) and Diana Dors (above) who was launched gondola-wise in a £150 mink number at the Venice film fest of 1955.

Hollywood didn't take long to realise the pay potential of this daring flashing of flesh, despite a conservative streak that went right through public life in the 50s and culminated in a strict self-censorship by the movie studios that made Brigitte's flamboyant (and seemingly natural) disrobing unthinkable on a US film set.

However, the barriers were there to come down, the bosoms (or portions of them) and bottoms would eventually be bared, and it took pioneers like Jayne Mansfield, the B-movie-ubiquitous Mamie Van Doren and glamour model Bettie Page to do just that.

Jayne Mansfield (left) was the 'Girl Can't Help It' bombshell who seemed to do more photo sessions than films, and whose figure was almost literally over the top most of the time. Although unfairly likened to a 'poor man's Marilyn', there was very little ambition to being the serious actress with Ms Mansfield; Jayne just loved publicity, and the myriad bikini picture-calls provided lots of that. She even helped market a line of JM-in-bikini hot water bottles (see page 3) which are now collectors' classics.

Mamie Van Doren was the femme fatale of a dozen scorching second features including such teen-teaser epics as 'High School Confidential', 'Girls Town', 'Untamed Youth' and her all-time critical low 'Sex Kittens Go To College'. Well into her late twenties when she made these kitsch classics in the late 50s, she was happy to be cast as the rebellious teenage sex-pot, balancing her youth-cult status in the movies – more often than not in tight-sweater-and-jeans roles – with adult acceptance through the pages of the glamour mags, where she was usually to be found bikini clad – or less.

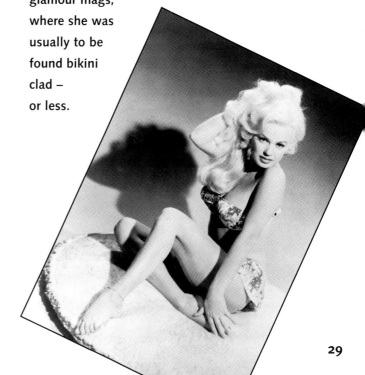

"These photos were taken on a camera club trip to a farm in New Jersey. I made most of my swim suits and this bikini was no exception. How do you like those stockings and high heels down on the farm?"

Bettie Page, USA 1996

Bettie Page was the undisputed Queen of the Glamour Girls, the precursors of Playboy Playmates and Penthouse Pets who decorated the pages of male-appeal glam magazines in the 1950s. Although it involved unpretentious shots for a news-stand public, photographers like Irving Klaw and Bunny Yeager made art out of their craft, and Bettie was their favourite – and certainly their most celebrated – subject.

SIXTIES A GO-GO

The 1960s were kooky, kinky and krazy, or so we were told at the time . . .

FUN FUN FUN!

Once Hollywood cottoned on to the bikini there was no stopping it. The early 1960s saw a rash of squeaky-clean teen-oriented beach movies, largely inspired by the surfing music of Jan and Dean, the Surfaris and the Beach Boys, and usually starring Annette Funicello. The bikini was now deemed safe; fun-loving college kids romped across the sands of California in such marina masterpieces as 'Bikini Beach', 'Beach Party' and not forgetting the marvellously-titled 'How To Stuff A Wild Bikini'. Surf's up!

THE "BEACH PARTY" gang goes DRAGSTRIP!

...IT'S WHERE THE GIRLS ARE BARE-ING
THE GUYS ARE DAR-ING AND
THE SURFS RARE-ING
TO GO-GO-GO!

AMERICAN INTERNATIONAL presents in PANAVISION and PATHECOLOR

Bikini Beach

FRANKIE AVALON • "ANNETTE" FUNICELLO • MARTHA HYER • HARVEY LEMBECK • DON RICKLES • JOHN ASHLEY
JODY McCREA • CANDY JOHNSON • LITTLE STEVIE WONDER • THE PYRAMIDS • William Asher • KEENAN WYNN
WILLIAM ASHER • LEO TOWNSEND • ROBERT DILLON • JAMES H. NICHOLSON • SAMUEL Z. ARKOFF

AMERICAN INTERNATIONAL STARS BOB CUMMINGS IN
THAT SWINGIN' TWISTIN' SURFIN'...
BEACH PARTY

DOROTHY MALONE • FRANKIE AVALON • ANNETTE FUNICELLO • HARVEY LEMBECK • JODY McCREA • JOHN ASHLEY

ALSO STARRING MOREY AMSTERDAM • AND EVA SIX • AND FEATURING DICK DALE AND THE DEL TONES • Directed by WILLIAM ASHER • Written by LOU RUSOFF • Produced by JAMES H. NICHOLSON and LOU RUSOFF • Executive Producer SAMUEL Z. ARKOFF • Music by LES BAXTER in PATHECOLOR AND PANAVISION • 6 NEW SURFIN' HITS

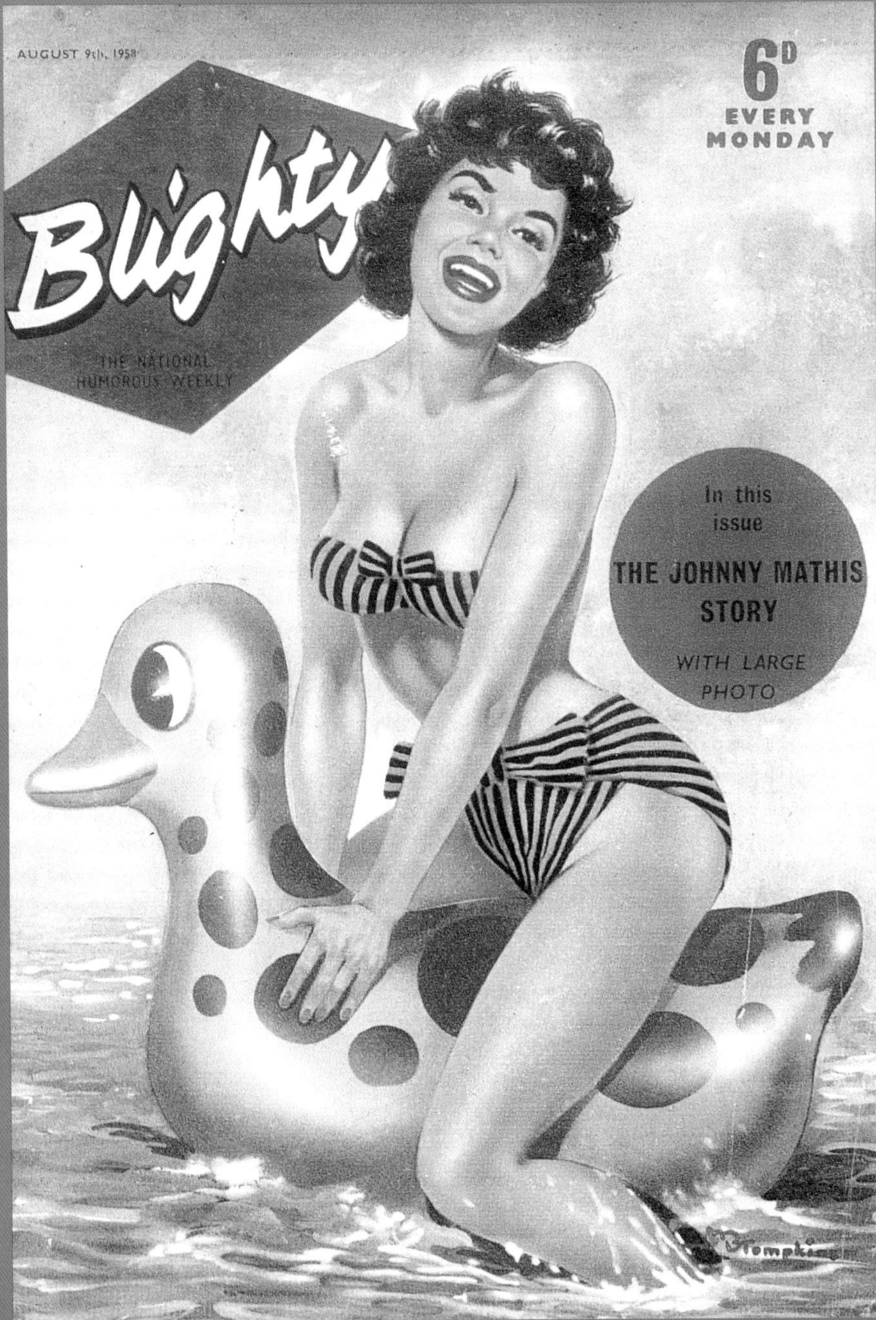

AUGUST 9th, 1958

6D
EVERY
MONDAY

Blighty

THE NATIONAL
HUMOROUS WEEKLY

In this
issue

**THE JOHNNY MATHIS
STORY**

*WITH LARGE
PHOTO*

Vacation-wise, the 60s marked the end of one era and the start of another. In the UK, holidays in the sun would still mean wind-blown British seaside resorts for most people, though mass migrations of sun searchers to Spain, Greece and further abroad were just around the corner. But in the Swingin' decade the bikini made its initial, tentative mark in the cosier – though chillingly inappropriate – climes of Blackpool, Brighton and the Butlin chain of holiday camps.

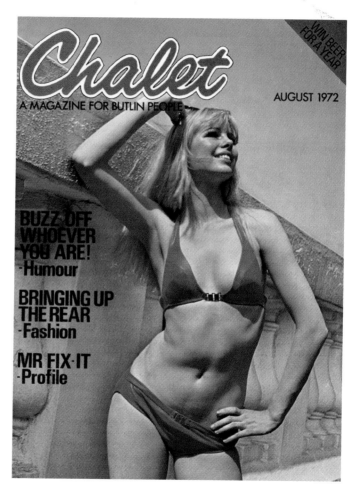

Chalet

A MAGAZINE FOR BUTLIN PEOPLE

AUGUST 1972

WIN BEER FOR A YEAR

BUZZ OFF WHOEVER YOU ARE! -Humour

BRINGING UP THE REAR -Fashion

MR FIX-IT -Profile

YES, EMMA, IT'S A LOVELY VIEW

"What a smashing naval display!"

BATHING BEAUTY CONTEST

British 'end of the pier' humour, full of nudge-nudge and the double entendre, was bound to make the most of the bikini's possibilities, be it in traditional seaside postcards or the long line of 'Carry On' films which provided belly laughs of the boob-and-bottom variety for over 30 years.

Barbara Windsor about to lose her top in 'Carry On Camping'

M-G-M presents in association with
SEVEN ARTS PRODUCTIONS
James B. Harris and Stanley Kubrick's "LOLITA"

Copyright ©1962 Metro-Goldwyn-Mayer Inc.

Vladimir Nabokov's book 'Lolita' introduced the child-woman 'nymphet' that had been hinted at by the teenage Bardot back in the early 50s, and Stanley Kubrick's film handled the subject with an absence of prurience that addressed the serious issues of the original. Of course, that didn't stop the studios making the most of actress Sue Lyon's bikini-kid image when it came to the movie's publicity.

LO07 OUT! HERE COMES THE BIGGEST BOND OF ALL!

HARRY SALTZMAN and ALBERT R. BROCCOLI present

SEAN CONNERY

in IAN FLEMING'S

"THUNDERBALL"

Bond guys Sean Connery (top) and Roger Moore,
with assorted Bond girls

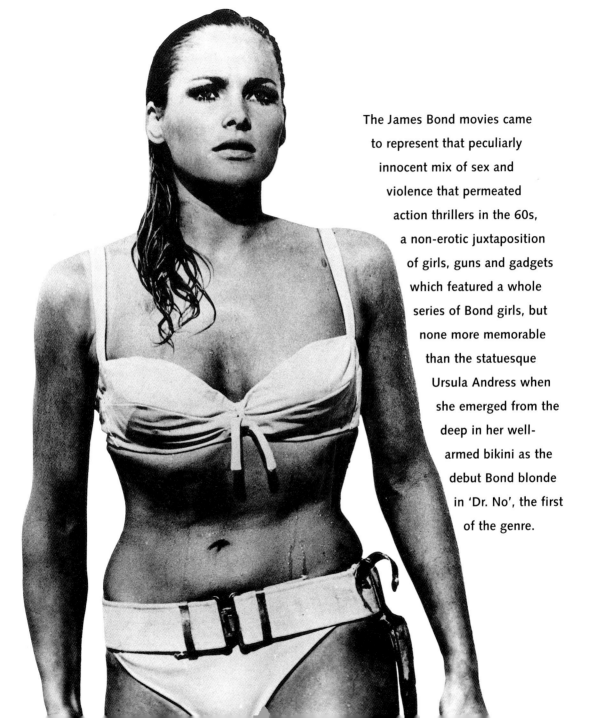

The James Bond movies came to represent that peculiarly innocent mix of sex and violence that permeated action thrillers in the 60s, a non-erotic juxtaposition of girls, guns and gadgets which featured a whole series of Bond girls, but none more memorable than the statuesque Ursula Andress when she emerged from the deep in her well-armed bikini as the debut Bond blonde in 'Dr. No', the first of the genre.

41

ASSOCIATED BRITISH-PATHE Presents A HAMMER FILM Production

ON!
MILLIO
YEARS B.

Starring RAQUEL WELCH · JOHN RICH

with PERCY HERBERT · ROBERT BROWN · MARTIN

Special Visual Effects Created by RAY HARRYHAUSEN · Music and Special Musical Effects Composed by MARIO NASCIMBENE · Screenplay by MICHAEL CARRERAS · Adapted from an original screenplay by Mickell Novak, George Baker, Joseph Frickert · Associate Producer AIDA YOUNG · Produced by MICHAEL CARRERAS · Directed by DON CHAFFEY · TECH

More fantastic than Bond were the exploits of the scantily-dressed 'Barbarella', a space-age cartoon brought to the screen by Roger Vadim, featuring a can't-say-no Jane Fonda heroine who would now be deemed very politically incorrect indeed. And not a million light years away (below), a galaxy of girls in the 1990s exploiter epic 'Space Zombie Bingo!!!'

Prehistoric monster movies through the ages – from Fay Wray's close shave with assorted dinosaurs in 'King Kong' – invariably teamed the brontosaurial Beast with a breathless Beauty, none more memorably than 'One Million Years BC' (left) which brought the fur bikini into its own via Raquel Welsh, whose dialogue was even more minimal than the animal-skin swimwear.

American star Stella Stevens

A typically 60s model

RAZZLE-DAZZLE ONE PIECE 80/- IN PINK, BLUE OR BROWN. SIZES 32"–36".

MAGICAL BLACK BIKINI, 64/- ALSO IN WHITE, TURQUOISE, CERISE AND ROYAL. SIZES 32"–36".

Janet

WEAR-DATED SWIMSUITS ARE GUARANTEED BY MONSANTO FOR 1 YEAR'S NORMAL WEAR. MONEY BACK OR

...ese swimsuits peg out
we pay

The Ladybirds.

The talk of all the beaches from ...ate to Majorca this summer is going to ...about a brand new species of ...suit called Miss LadyBird. ...Holidays have never been so ...fully packaged. Ten new styles ...anning Bri-Nylon. ...Bikini and one-piece. Stretch fabric. ...The shape is up to the Ladybird inside ...is only natural. ...But it's colours and patterns that will

really put Miss LadyBirds rivals in the shade.
(There is a rumour going round that Ladybird watching will replace all other forms of water sport.)
Any girl-size girl 32, 34, 36, 38 bust who admits her age to be somewhere between 16 and 26, will make a lovely Ladybird.
Miss LadyBird is to be found in your local shop.
With stockists all round the country (part of our careful strategy that preceded

this announcement) we can safely say
And at a selling price of around
Miss LadyBird is going to be as popu...
with the girls as she is with the boys.
Included in the price is a specia...
hanger-bag for carrying all Ladybird...
like tanning cream and spare sunglas...
perhaps another Miss LadyBird to c...
into after swimming.
Miss LadyBird the best name fo...
quality and value. **Miss LadyBird**
For all the Ladybirds

BRI NYLON

BRI-NYLON is a Registered Trade Mark of ICI.

Left: Dorothy Perkins reversible bikini in Vincel/cotton, about £2.99   Right: Dorothy Perkins shirred bikini in Vincel/cotton, about £2.99

Cool it. The name of the game is Vincel.

Feel cool. Feel free. te Vincel. There's a whole lot that's new this Spring –
easy to look at, easy to look after. For clothes that know what it's all about, go for
breathe-easy Vincel. It's the name of the game.

STOCKISTS

COURTAULDS Vincel

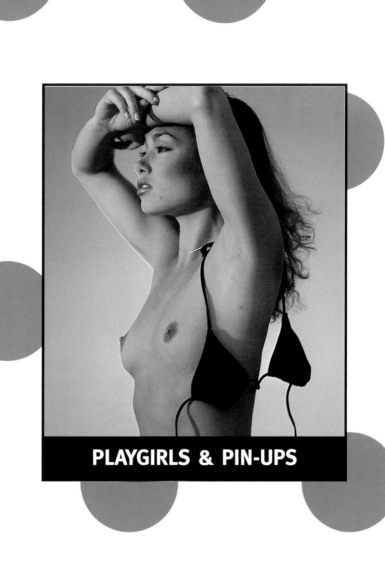

PLAYGIRLS & PIN-UPS

Into the 70s and the bikini featured on ever more sophisticated glamour photography. Soft-focus nudity verging on soft-porn had taken over a large part of the traditional men's magazines, consequently 'clothed' sessions, bikini or otherwise, were consciously more 'arty' in their approach, just at a time when fashion designers and fashion photographers were including the bikini more and more in their work, and it began to appear in the fashion glossies more often than the girlie mags.

That seemingly male-driven world of the motor trade has been notorious in its use of
female models to promote the apparent sexiness of fast cars – if they are that sexy, why
the need for the girls? – from the much-vaunted Pirelli calendar shoots to 'promotional'
models decorating the stands of motor shows world-wide.

When sword-and-sorcery reared its Viking-helmeted head in the 70s as a major fantasy genre, particularly in comic books, the most memorable female heroine was undoubtedly Marvel's Red Sonja, the 'She Devil With a Sword'.

Created by Robert E. Howard, the epically proportioned Sonja, wearing little more than her chain-mail bikini and trusty blade, vanquished enemies both human and otherwise. In 1985 Sonja was brought to the movie screen by the suitably Amazonian Brigitte Nielsen.

And all the time the bikini was actually getting smaller. In the mid 70s the briefest of bikinis

began to appear in various forms of mini-bikini that many saw as a sexually aggressive state-

ment on the part of the wearer. One psychologist went as far as to suggest that it was a way of

disguising shyness by women who lacked confidence in everything but their physical attributes.

Jamie Lee Curtis (here in her happy hooker role in 'Trading Places') and Jane Fonda in 'California Suite' were just two Hollywood stars who heralded the ever-more revealing styles of bikini becoming fashionable through the 70s and into the early 80s.

Designer Dreams

The 80s saw the culmination of the Beach Boom which had started a decade before. Rio de Janeiro's miles of beaches were where the locals as well as tourists were particularly noted for wearing the very least possible in the most noticeable way, and exotic destinations as far flung as India, South East Asia and the Caribbean were now crowded with holidaymakers, bikinied, topless and even nude, all worshipping the sun in an explosion of flesh which Louis Réard could only have half-imagined in that week of the atom bomb tests back in 1945.

Thongs and things: the increasing brevity of the bikini came in the form of the thong, the rikini, the loop and other exercises in the old conundrum 'how long is a piece of string?'

As minimalism spilled over from the bathing pool and beach onto the fashion catwalk, top designers including Hamnett, Versace, Ralph Lauren and Vivienne Westwood (opposite, top right) set out to confirm the old adage that less can some-times mean more, culminating (opposite, bottom right) in Karl Lagerfeld's sensational 1995 micro-bikini for Chanel.

Eva Hertzigova

Claudia Schiffer

Kate Moss

Helena Christensen

ACKNOWLEDGEMENTS

'Itsy Bitsy Teenie Weenie Yellow Polka Dot Bikini'
(Lee Pockriss, Paul J.Vance) Reproduced by
permission of **Campbell Connelly & Co.Ltd., London**

All jacket pictures courtesy of **Vintage Magazine
Company** except back inside flap, **Camera Press**
/Sam Levin

Advertising Archives 36, /Courtauld European Fibres
46, /Dupont (UK). Limited 45 right, /Jantzen Inc 11
centre, /Monsanto Services Int. 45 left.
Aquarius Picture Library 22, 27 background, 34, 38
bottom, 40 top, 40 bottom, 43 top.
Archive Photos 4 top, 16, 35 centre.
British Film Institute - Stills, Posters and Designs 35
bottom, 42 /43.
Black Star Stern 52 left, /Claus Meyer 57 bottom
centre, 57 bottom left, Claus Meyer 57 bottom right.
Butlins 37 top, 37 bottom.
Camera Press 45 bottom, 50, 61 right, /Allen Grant
3, /Sam Levin 23.
Glamorcon, Inc. 30 & 31.
Robert Harding Picture Library /FPG endpapers.
Historical Newspaper Loan Service 15 background.
Hulton Deutsch Collection 12 background, 13, 18
bottom, 26.
Image Bank /Amanda Clement 4 bottom, /Chris
Thomson 64.
Marc Kitchen-Smith 5.
Kobal Collection 24 left, 24 right, 28, 29,/American
International 35 top, MGM 39, 44 left /
Columbia/Ray Stark 53 right /Paramount 53 left.
Marvel 51.
Niall McInerney 58 bottom left, 58 top right, 60
right, 60 left, 61 left.
Phelan & Taylor Produce Co. (Oceano, California
93445) 6.
Popperfoto 11 bottom, 15 top, 18 centre.
Range Pictures Ltd 11 top, 18 top, /Bettman/UPI 14,
19, 27 centre.
Rex Features 52 right, /Sipa 58 top left.
Tony Stone Images 47, 49 bottom, /Roy Giles 48
/49, /Jon Gray 62 /63.
Sygma 20 /21, /Keystone 14 top, 15 bottom, /Pierre
Vauthey 58 bottom right, /James Andanson 56, 57
top right, 57 top left.
Topham 41.
Troma, Inc /Courtesy of Troma Studios 43 bottom.
Vintage Magazine Company 9, 12 foreground, 32,
38 centre, 38 top, 44 right, /Courtesy of Hearst
Magazine 25.